Alpha

Reprinted 2013, 2014



ISBN: 978 1 905887 96 5

*The authors and publisher gratefully acknowledge permission to reproduce copyright material in this book. Every effort has been made to trace and contact copyright holders. If there are any inadvertent omissions we apologise to those concerned and will ensure that a suitable acknowledgment is made in all future editions.*



Published by Alpha International, HTB Brompton Road, London, SW7 1JA.
Email: publications@alpha.org
Website: alpha.org

# Contents

# Welcome

We couldn't decide whether to call the first chapter 'Is There More to Life Than This?' or 'Christianity: Boring, Untrue, Irrelevant?' – they're both pretty big statements, and, naturally, we liked them for that reason, but at the end of the day it's difficult to know which one is the question that people are really asking, because everyone's asking something.

This guide outlines the contents of these and other big questions that are looked into on Alpha – Youth. Maybe one of them is the one you are asking, maybe you'll find your question answered on the way – whatever happens, this journey is about finding out what you and others around you think.

# Introductory Session

## Christianity: Boring, Untrue, Irrelevant?

# This is the 21st century. What on earth does Christianity have to offer me?

## Christianity: boring?

- Jesus says he came to give us life, and life to the full. Jesus said, 'I am … the life.' (John 14:6)
- Many people think that Christianity is about having no life. They believe that Christianity, and church in particular, is utterly boring
- Following Jesus is not only the most exciting way to live life to the fullest, but it is the reason you were created – it is why you are here. It's not meant to be boring!

## Christianity: untrue?

- Jesus said 'I am... the truth' (John 14:6) – not *a* truth, but *the* truth
- Truth isn't such a popular concept today. We speak of things being true 'for me' – and we are happy with the idea that one person's truth is another person's untruth
- But Christianity doesn't work that way. Its claims are so big that it must either be true for everyone, or true for no one. What it cannot be is true for some and not others

## Christianity: irrelevant?

- Jesus said, 'I am the way' (John 14:6). With Jesus to show us the way, we can have a life full of purpose, fun, direction and meaning
- With Jesus in our lives we become more like the people that God created us to be – Christianity is not the easiest way of life, but it is the most fulfilling

'What if you're a really good person, but you get into a really, really bad fight and your leg gets gangrene and it has to be amputated. Will it be waiting for you in heaven?'
**Bart Simpson**

'When you have eliminated the impossible, whatever remains, however improbable, must be the truth.'
**Arthur Conan Doyle, creator of Sherlock Holmes**

'I am an historian, I am not a believer, but I must confess as an historian that this penniless preacher from Nazareth is irrevocably the very centre of history. Jesus Christ is easily the most dominant figure in all history.'
**H. G. Wells, writer**

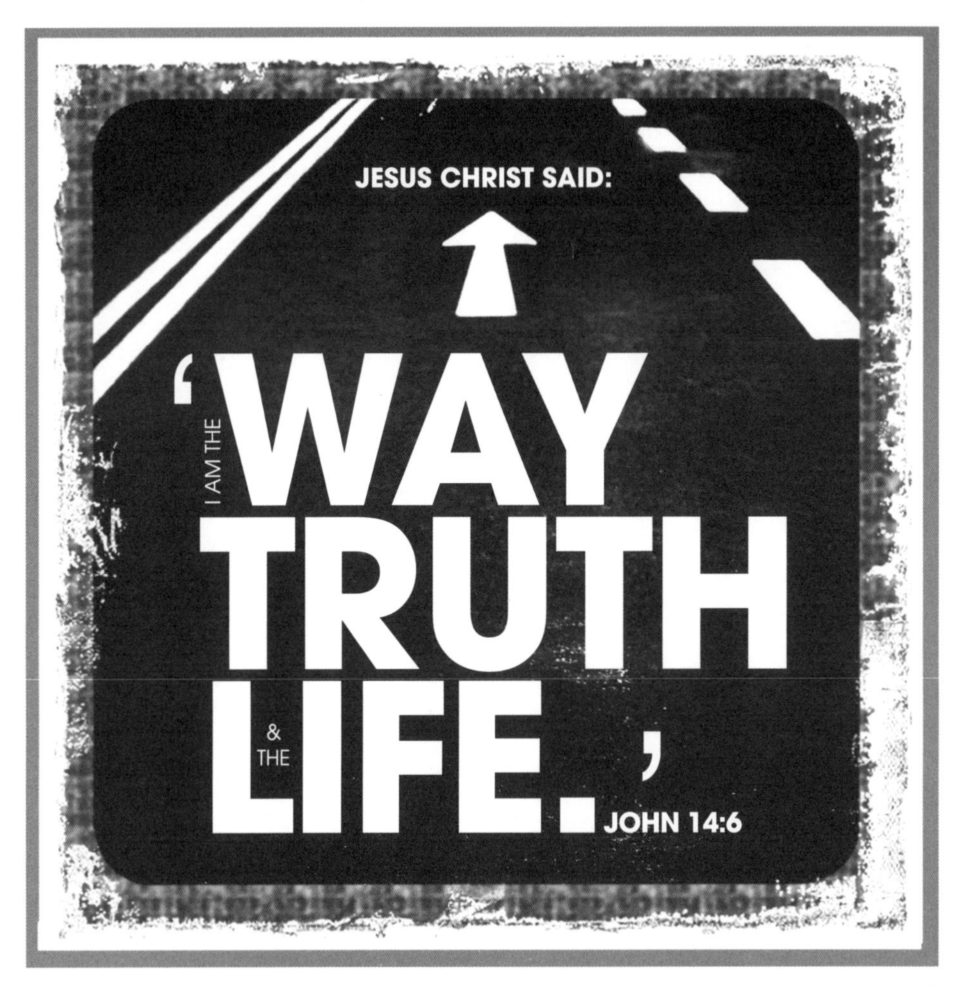
JESUS CHRIST SAID:
'I AM THE WAY TRUTH
& THE LIFE.'
JOHN 14:6

'If you could ask God one question, right now, what would it be?'
'If you could ask God one question, right now, what would it be?'
'If you could ask God one question, right now, what would it be?'
'If you could ask God one question, right now, what would it

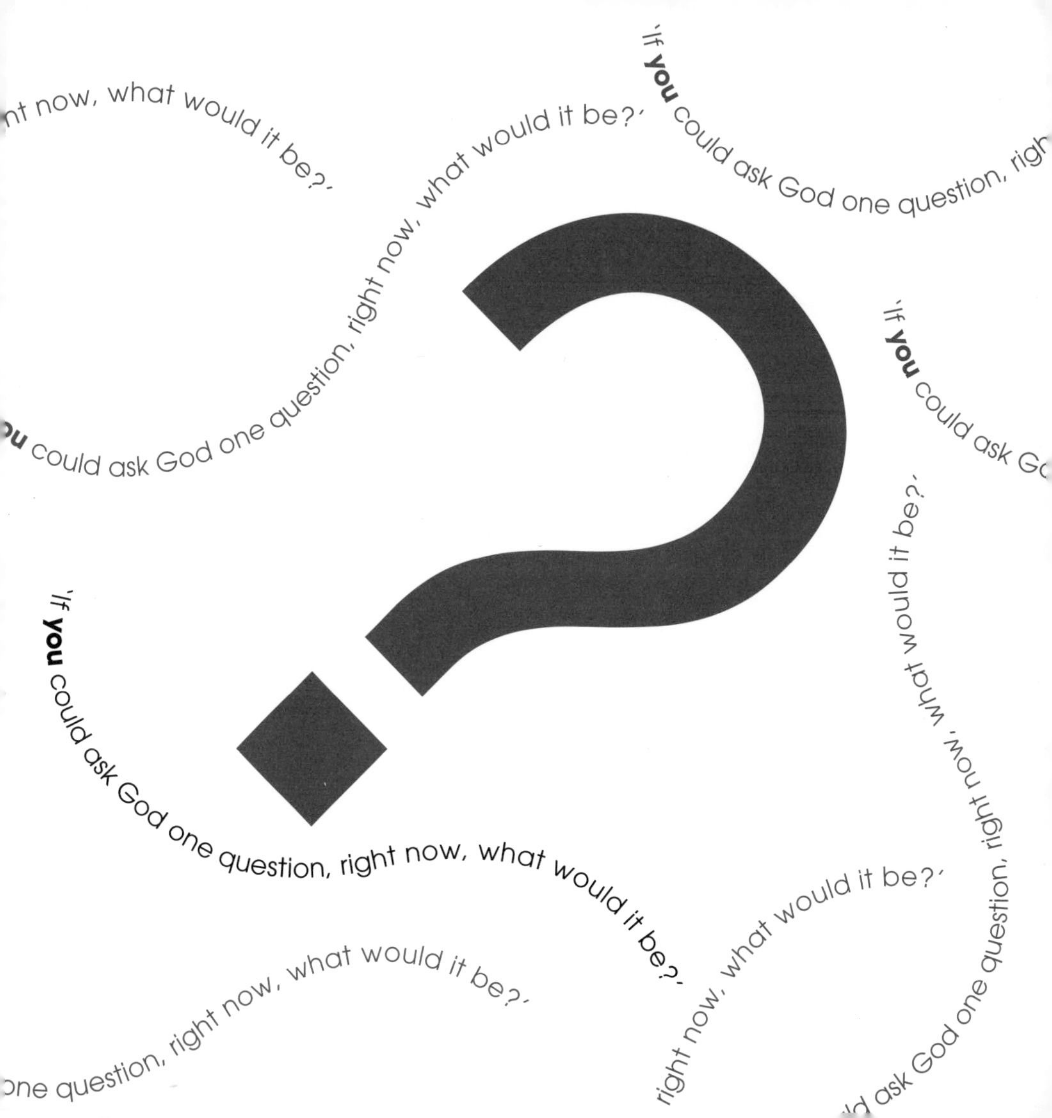
'If you could ask God one question, right now, what would it be?'
'If you could ask God one question, righ
nt now, what would it be?'
you could ask God one question, right now, what would it be?'
'If you could ask Go
ld ask God one question, right now, what would it be?'
right now, what would it be?'
one question, right now, what would it be?'

## Going Deeper: Drawing The Wrong Conclusion

An English lady wanted to buy a house in Switzerland. Following a viewing of the perfect property, she realised that she hadn't seen a toilet there. She wrote to the Swiss estate agent, and enquired about the location of the 'WC' (an old English abbreviation for 'water closet' – a polite way of saying toilet!).

The estate agent's knowledge of English was limited, so he asked the parish priest to translate the letter for him. The only meaning for the abbreviation 'WC' that the priest could think of was either Wayside Chapel or Wesleyan Chapel. As a result, the reply sent from the estate agent read:

'My Dear Madam,

I take great pleasure in informing you that the WC is situated nine miles from the house in a beautiful grove of pine trees surrounded by lovely grounds. It is capable of holding 229 people and it is open on Sundays and Thursdays only. As there are a great number of people expected during the summer months, it is an unfortunate situation, especially if you are in the habit of going regularly. It may interest you to know that my daughter was married in the WC and it was there that she met her husband. I can remember the rush there was for seats. There were ten people to every seat usually occupied by one.

You will be glad to hear that a good number of people bring their lunch and make a day of it, while those who can afford to go by car arrive just in time. I would especially recommend your ladyship to go on Thursdays when there is an organ accompaniment.

The acoustics are excellent, even the most delicate sounds can be heard everywhere.

The newest addition is a bell donated by a wealthy resident of the district. It rings every time a person enters. A bazaar is to be held to provide plush seats for all, since the people feel it is long needed. My wife is rather delicate and she cannot attend regularly. It is almost a year since she went last, and naturally it pains her very much not to be able to go more often. I shall be delighted to reserve the best seat for you, where you shall be seen by all. For the children, there is a special day and time so that they do not disturb the elders. Hoping to be of some service to you. Yours faithfully, etc...'

*It is easy to get the wrong idea from limited information. Many people have come to the conclusion that church and Christianity is irrelevant to their lives, but what if they have jumped to the wrong conclusion?*

# Session 1
# Who is Jesus?

# What is it about Jesus that leads people to continue talking about him over 2,000 years after he lived?

## Did Jesus Actually Exist?

Most scholars, whether Christians or not, agree that the following points are true about the life of Jesus Christ:

- He was a Jewish man, born in Bethlehem in Judea around 4 BC
- He was famous for being a great teacher and miracle worker
- He was crucified by the Roman authorities
- His followers believed he was the Son of God and that he rose from the dead

## Was Jesus More Than Just a 'Good Man'?

So who did Jesus think he was? He made some pretty big claims:

- He claimed to be the Son of God (Mark 14:61–2). He said that anyone who had seen him had seen God (John 14:9). He said 'I am the resurrection and the life' (meaning he would overcome death and give us eternal life, John 11:25)
- He claimed that he could forgive sin – in Mark 2:5 he said to someone, 'Your sins are forgiven.' People knew that only God could forgive sins

So what if Jesus was wrong? Logically we would have three options:

1. Jesus wasn't God, and knew he wasn't, so he was lying: **he was a fraudster, an evil, deceptive person**
2. Jesus wasn't God but thought he was: **he was genuine, but deluded. He was insane**
3. Jesus was telling the truth: **he is God**

What do you think? Mad, bad or God?

# Is There Any Evidence to Support Jesus' Claims?

- What Jesus taught is generally accepted as the best teaching ever. The miracles and healings he performed, and the way he lived his life, support his claims
- He was so perfect that his enemies couldn't find anything of which to convict him
- Jesus' fulfillment of 300 Old Testament prophecies about things like his birth, mother, death and burial, supports his claims: 29 were fulfilled in a single day!
- Jesus' resurrection from the dead supports his claims. If true, it is proof he is God. The physical resurrection of Jesus is the cornerstone of Christianity

'I would like to ask him if he was indeed virgin born, because the answer to that question would define history.'

**Larry King, television interviewer and presenter**

'A man who was merely a man and said the sort of things Jesus said wouldn't be a great moral teacher; he'd either be insane or else he'd be the devil of hell. You must make your choice. Either this man was and is the Son of God or else insane or something worse. But don't let us come up with any patronising nonsense about his being a great human teacher. He hasn't left that open to us. He didn't intend to.'

**C. S. Lewis, author of the 'Narnia' books**

'The secular response to the Christian story always goes like this: [Jesus] was a great prophet, obviously a very interesting guy … But actually Christ doesn't allow you that. He doesn't let you off that hook. Christ says "I am God incarnate" … So what you are left with is either Christ was who he said he was or a complete nutcase.'

**Bono, lead singer of U2**

'No one else holds or has held the place in the heart of the world which Jesus holds. Other gods have been as devoutly worshipped; no other man has been so devoutly loved.'

**John Knox, Scottish preacher**

JESUS SAID
'I have come
that they may have life, and have it to the
FULL'
John 10:10

WHO DO YOU

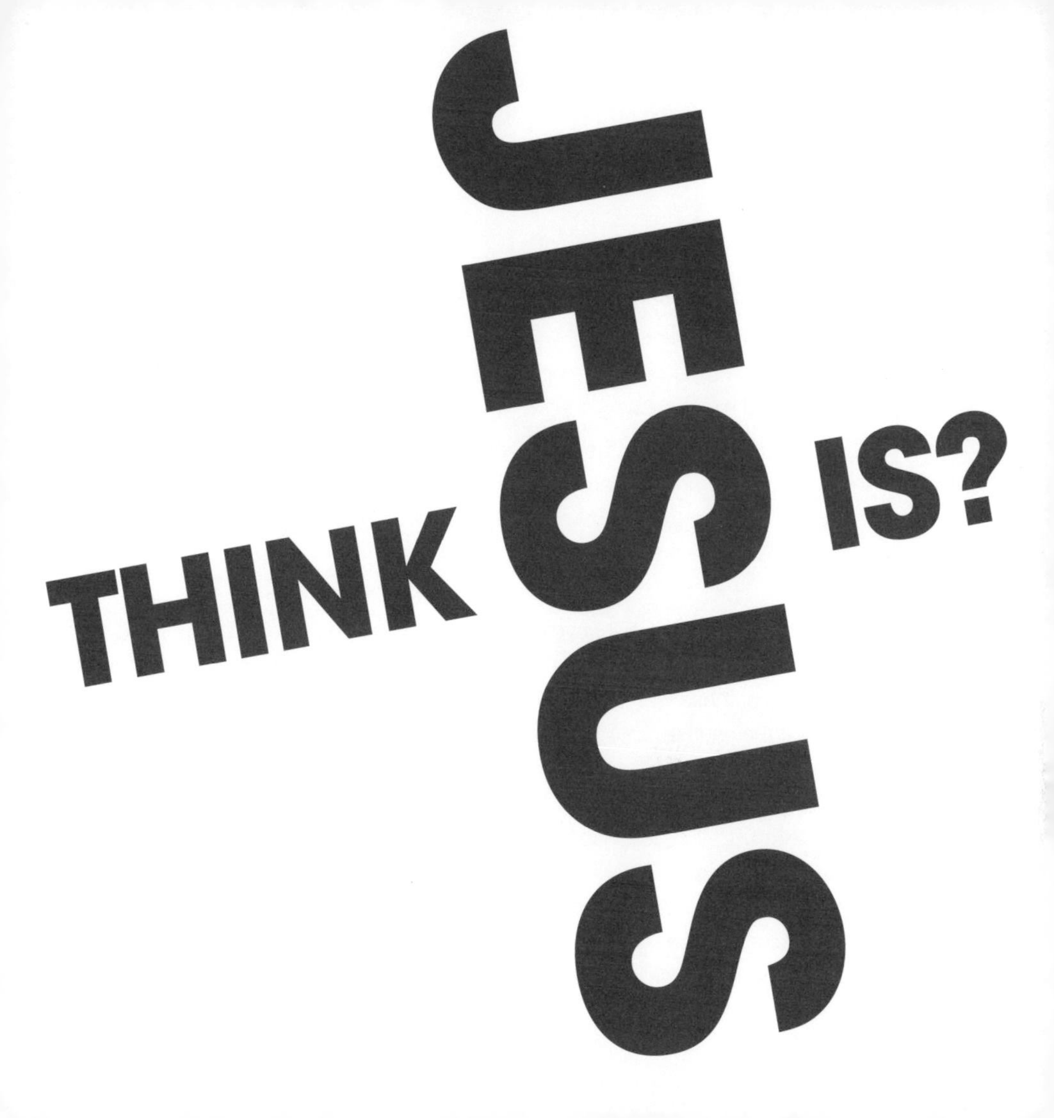
THINK
JESUS
IS?

## Going Deeper: Textual Criticism

Through the science of textual criticism, we know that versions of the Bible through the ages have remained true to the original copy – they are more accurate than the copies of other well-respected historical works.

Textual criticism can determine whether the copies of ancient texts we read now are the same as when they were written. There are two main questions to ask in order to find out:

1. How quickly after the original was written was the earliest copy made?
2. How many copies are there?

So:

- Histories by Herodotus and Thucydides were both written in the 5th century BC. The earliest copies that we have are from around AD 900, so there's a 1,300-year gap. For each of these works we have only eight copies but no classical scholar would doubt their authenticity
- *Histories* by Tacitus: 1,000-year gap between the original and the first copy; a total of twenty copies
- Caesar's *Gallic War*: 950-year gap between the original and the first copy; a total of nine or ten copies etc... you get the idea
- The New Testament: written between 40 and 100 AD. The earliest copy we have is AD 130, and we have full manuscripts at AD 350. So, at most, there's a 310-year gap. And we have: 5,309 Greek manuscripts, 10,000 Latin manuscripts and 9,300 others

| WORK | WHEN WRITTEN | EARLIEST COPY | TIME LAPSE | COPIES |
|---|---|---|---|---|
| Herodotus | 488–428 BC | AD 900 | 1,300 years | 8 |
| Thucydides | c.460–400 BC | AD 900 | 1,300 years | 8 |
| Tacitus | AD 100 | AD 1,100 | 1,000 years | 20 |
| Caesar's *Gallic War* | 58–50 BC | AD 900 | 950 years | 9–10 |
| Livy's *Roman History* | 59 BC–AD 17 | AD 900 | 900 years | 20 |
| New Testament | AD 40–100 | AD 130 (full manuscripts AD 350) | 30–310 years | 5,000+ Greek<br>10,000 Latin<br>9,300 others |

# Session 2
# Why Did Jesus Die?

# Why would anyone wear an instrument of death and torture as jewellery?

## What's the Problem?

- God made the world and designed us to be in relationship with him. What he really wants is to have a friendship, a perfect relationship, with us
- God created us perfect, or clean, like a new, spotless white t-shirt. As long as we are clean, we can have a relationship with him
- But the problem is that none of us, not one, is perfect – all of us have 'sinned' (done wrong). We've 'messed up the t-shirt'. And this mess separates us from God

## What's the Solution?

- God's son, Jesus, was the only human to ever live a perfect life
- When Jesus died, he died the death that each of us deserved – the death that we would have had to die, because we have fallen short of God's standards. Jesus died in our place, and gave us his own sinlessness, his 'clean t-shirt', to live in
- Because Jesus took our sin upon himself, it means we can have a relationship with God – Jesus has taken away the separation caused by our sin

## What's the Result?

- Jesus came through death and was resurrected – he conquered death. This means that we don't need to fear death. Jesus' death and resurrection gives us eternal life
- On the cross, Jesus paid for all of our debts. Jesus said: 'If the Son sets you free, you will be free indeed' (John 8:36)
- So all we need to do is recognise it – if we believe that Jesus suffered on the cross for us, and if we say sorry for the things that we have done wrong (our sins), we can begin to know God and have that relationship with him

'If the resurrection is not true, Christianity becomes null and void.'

**Richard Dawkins, biologist and author**

'A man who was completely innocent, offered himself as a sacrifice for the good of others, including his enemies, and became the ransom of the world. It was a perfect act.'

**Mahatma Gandhi**

'I know men and I tell you that Jesus Christ is no mere man. Between him and every person in the world there is no possible term of comparison. Alexander, Caesar, Charlemagne and I have founded empires. But on what did we rest the creation of our genius? Upon force. Jesus Christ founded his empire upon love; and at this hour millions of men would die for him.'

**Napoleon, French emperor 1804–1815**

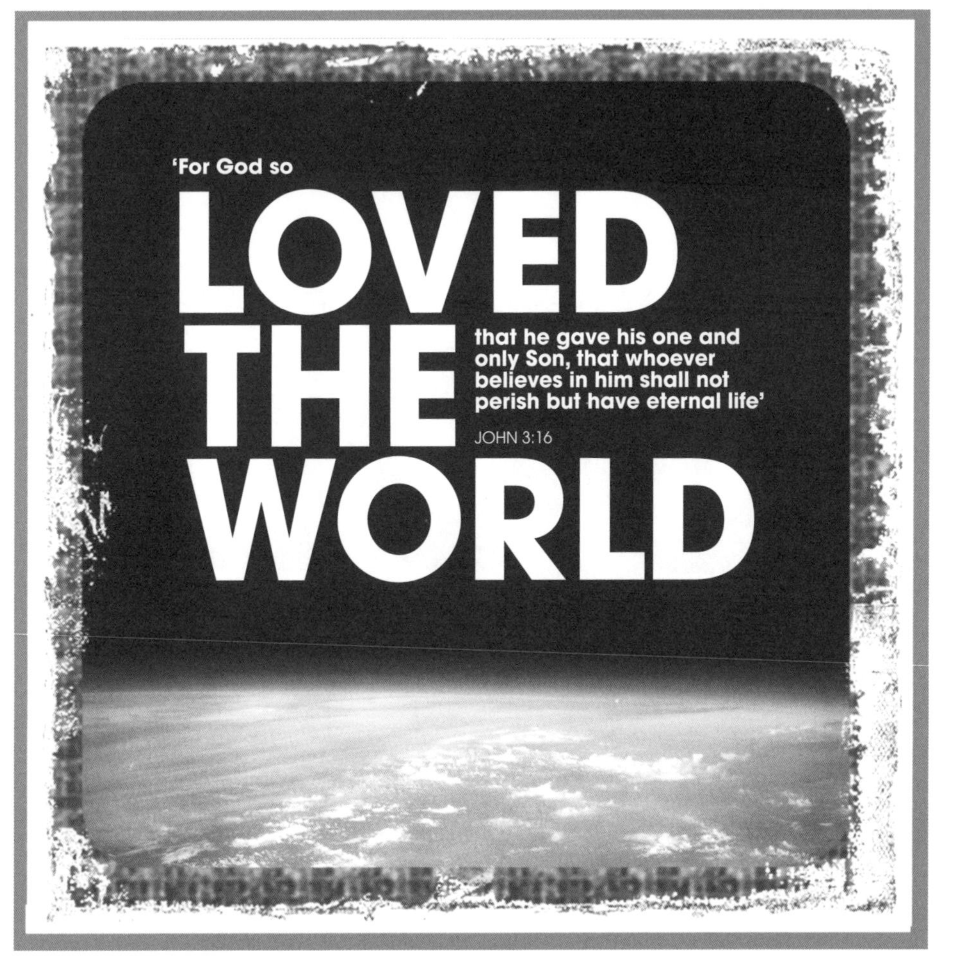
'For God so
LOVED
THE
WORLD
that he gave his one and only Son, that whoever believes in him shall not perish but have eternal life'
JOHN 3:16

HOW DO YOU FEEL ABOUT THE IDEA THAT

WANTS TO BE IN RELATIONSHIP WITH YOU?

## Going Deeper: Crucifixion

Cicero, a Roman philosopher, lawyer and poltician (106 BC–43 BC), described crucifixion as 'the most cruel and hideous of tortures. Jesus was stripped and tied to a whipping-post, he was flogged with four or five strips of leather interwoven with sharp, jagged bone and lead.'

Eusebius, the third-century historian, described Roman flogging in these terms: 'The sufferer's veins were laid bare, and the very muscles, sinews and bowels of the victim were opened to exposure. He was then taken to the Praetorium, where a crown of thorns was thrust on his head. He was forced to carry a heavy crossbar on his bleeding shoulders until he collapsed.

When they reached the site of crucifixion he was again stripped naked. He was laid on the cross and six-inch nails were driven into his forearms just above the wrists. His knees were then twisted sideways so that the ankles could be nailed between the tibia and the Achilles tendon. He was lifted up on the cross, which was then dropped into a socket in the ground. There he was left to hang in intense heat and unbearable thirst, exposed to the ridicule of the crowd. He hung there, in unthinkable pain, for six hours while his life slowly drained away. It was the height of pain and depth of shame.'

# Session 3
# How Can We Have Faith?

# Does going to church make you a Christian? How can we know that our faith is based on something more than just a fairytale?

Our confidence in our faith can be based upon three things. They are the Father, the Son, and the Holy Spirit – this is called the 'Trinity'.

## What the Father Promises

- We have God's written word – the Bible. This is a written record of his love for us and commitment to us. If, at any point, we aren't *feeling* loved, we can *know* that God loves us because it says so in the Bible
- In the Bible, God promises that he will come in to our lives if we ask him

So if you have sincerely asked him to come in, you can be *sure* he has. Jesus doesn't force anyone to let him into their lives – the choice is ours.

- God promises that he will be with us forever (Matthew 28:20) and to give us eternal life with him in heaven (John 10:28)
- Faith is taking God's promises and daring to believe them

## What Jesus Did

- Jesus was unique. He saved us when we couldn't save ourselves: he made a relationship with God possible for us
- We can never earn God's forgiveness, but Jesus died to destroy the barrier that sin creates between us and God

## What the Spirit Does

- Whenever someone becomes a Christian, God's Holy Spirit comes to live within them (Romans 8:9)
- When the Holy Spirit lives in us, we begin to live and act more like Jesus. This is described in the Bible as the 'fruit' of the Holy Spirit (Galatians 5:22). It doesn't happen overnight, but over time – like fruit growing
- Having God's Holy Spirit in us helps us to know for certain that he loves us

## Conclusion

- Becoming a Christian involves faith, but not blind faith.
- We can trust in the promises of God in the Bible, we can look to the cross and see his love for us, and we can know God through his Holy Spirit living inside us

Our feelings go up and down depending on the day, the week and the mood we're in.

But we don't base our faith on how we are feeling day-by-day, although that is important. We can base our faith on what God promises us in the Bible.

'Faith is to believe what you do not see; the reward of this faith is to see what you believe.'
**Saint Augustine**

'Faith is not belief without proof, but trust without reservation.'
**D. Elton Trueblood, American author and theologian**

'To one who has faith, no explanation is necessary. To one without faith, no explanation is possible.'
**Thomas Aquinas, philosopher and theologian**

'DO YOU NOT **KNOW**? HAVE YOU NOT **HEARD**?
THE LORD IS THE

# EVERLASTING GOD

THE **CREATOR OF THE ENDS OF THE EARTH**.
HE WILL NOT GROW TIRED OR WEARY, AND HIS UNDERSTANDING NO-ONE CAN FATHOM.'

ISAIAH 40:28

CAN YOU TRUST YOUR FEELINGS
OR IS THERE MORE TO MAKING A DECISION THAN THAT?

## Going Deeper: Lean Upon

John Patton was a Scot who travelled all the way from Scotland to a group of islands in the South West Pacific in order to tell the tribal people about Jesus. He wanted to translate the Bible into their tribal language.

The islanders were cannibals and his life was in constant danger. When Patton tried to translate the Bible into the tribal language he found there was no word for 'belief' or 'trust'. Nobody trusted anybody else.

Finally, when one of the tribal people came in to his study, he thought of a way to find the word he was looking for. Patton raised both his feet off of the ground, leant back in his chair and asked the man, 'What am I doing now?' The servant gave him a word, which means 'to lean your whole weight upon'. This was the word Patton used in his translation of the Bible.

That's what faith is – leaning our entire weight on God.

# Session 4
# Why and How Do I Pray?

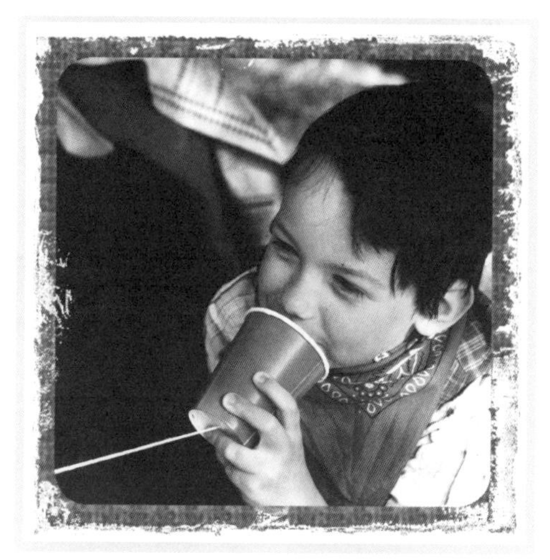

# Often, when bad things happen, people turn to prayer. Why is that?

## What is Prayer?

- Prayer is like having a 'hotline' to God
- We pray:
  - to the Father – God is our 'dad', but he is also holy and powerful (Matthew 6:6)
  - through the Son – Jesus is always our link to God the Father (Ephesians 2:18)
  - by the Holy Spirit – the Holy Spirit helps us to pray (Romans 8:26)

## Why Pray?

- Jesus prayed – and told us to do the same (Mark 1:35; Luke 6:12, 9:18, 9:28, 11:1)
- It's how we develop a relationship with God – friendship is grown by spending time together
- It brings us joy and peace – even in difficult times (John 16:24; Philippians 4:6–7)
- It changes situations – prayer works (Matthew 7:7–11)

## Does God Always Answer My Prayers?

- Yes, but not always in the way we ask him to. God may say yes, no or wait ...
- Sometimes God cannot answer all prayers with a 'yes', because it is impossible. Both teams can't win the same match!
- Other times, God says 'no' or 'wait', because the prayers we pray are not good for us, and he knows better than we do (Matthew 7:11)
- Sometimes he doesn't answer our prayers because we can let things create a barrier between ourselves and God. Perhaps if we have been disobedient (1 John 3:21–22), don't forgive others (Matthew 6:14–15), if we haven't said sorry to God for the things we have done wrong (Isaiah 59:2), or if our motives are wrong (James 4:2–3)

## How To Pray

We can pray anytime, anywhere. To help us to pray we can follow a pattern:

**S – sorry:** apologise to God for what you have done wrong

**T – thank you:** praise God for all he has given you

**P – please:** ask God for what you, and others, need

'Pray, and let God worry.'

**Martin Luther, German priest and scholar**

'I have been driven many times to my knees by the overwhelming conviction that I had absolutely no other place to go.'

**Abraham Lincoln, US President 1861–1865**

'When I pray, coincidences happen, and when I don't pray, they don't.'

**William Temple, former Archbishop of Canterbury**

Jesus said: 'This, then, is how you should pray:
OUR
FATHER
IN HEAVEN,
hallowed be your name,
your kingdom come, your will be done on earth as it is in heaven.
Give us today our daily bread.
Forgive us our debts,
as we also have forgiven our debtors.
And lead us not into temptation,
but deliver us from the evil one.'
MATTHEW 6: 9–13

What do you find most attractive about the idea of

# PRAYER?

# Going Deeper: The Power of Persistent Prayer

A Christian named Monica was having real problems with her rebellious teenage son. He was lazy, bad-tempered, a cheat, a liar and a thief. Although he went on to become a very respectable lawyer, his life was dominated by worldly ambition and a desire to make money. His morals were 'loose' (as they would say in old English). He lived with several different women and had a son by one of them. At one stage, he joined a weird religious cult and adopted all kinds of strange practices.

Throughout this time, his mother continued to pray for him. One day, the Lord gave her a vision. She wept as she prayed, because she saw the light of Christ shining on her son; his face was smiling at her with great joy. This encouraged her to keep on praying. It was nine years before her son finally gave his life to Christ, at the age of twenty-eight.

That man's name was Augustine, now known as Saint Augustine: he became a Christian in 386 AD, was ordained in 391, made a bishop in 396, and is perhaps the greatest theologian of the church ever.

Saint Augustine always attributed his conversion to the prayers of his mother. Her prayers literally changed the course of history. Prayer is a very powerful thing!

# Session 5
# Why and How Should I Read the Bible?

# How can a book that dates from around 2,000 years ago still have any relevance to our lives in the 21st century?

## An instruction manual for life

- The Bible is the story of God, his love for the world and the humans who live in it. All the elements that make soap operas and films so gripping also appear in the Bible. There is sex, romance, war, revenge, love, sacrifice and murder
- This is no ordinary book. The Bible is uniquely God's book. It is 'God-breathed' or 'God-inspired'. Even though humans wrote the words, it was God who inspired and guided them (2 Timothy 3:15–17)
- God has designed the Bible to be much more like a compass than a map. This is why it is still useful today when showing us how best to live our lives. It provides us with principles that don't change with time, and that can help us to make all kinds of decisions

## A way to relationship

- If the Bible was just an instruction manual, it might seem a bit cold and boring, like a very big, very thick textbook
- But written communications can lead to real relationship. God speaks to us and builds a relationship with us primarily through the Bible. It is like a love letter, a text message (or several), and an email all rolled into one

## How do we hear God speak through the Bible?

- It's hard to hear God when there are lots of other voices shouting – the right conditions are important in any form of communication
- So choose a place where you are relaxed and where you won't be disturbed or get distracted. Begin by praying – ask God to speak to you through what you read
- Ask yourself three key questions about the text: What does this say? What does this mean? How should this affect me?
- Put what you have read and learned into practice (Matthew 7:24). And most of all enjoy it!

gideons.org.uk

'As a child I received instruction both in the Bible and in the Talmud. I am a Jew, but I am enthralled by the luminous figure of the Nazarene … No one can read the Gospels without feeling the actual presence of Jesus.'
**Albert Einstein, scientist**

Some rights reserved by James Vaughan

'By your words I can see where I'm going; they throw a beam of light on my dark path.'
**Psalm 119:105, The Message Bible**

The Bible tops the bestseller list with between 2.5 billion and 6 billion copies sold – why is it so popular?

'I have a fundamental belief in the Bible as the Word of God, written by men who were inspired. I study the Bible daily.'
**Sir Isaac Newton, scientist**

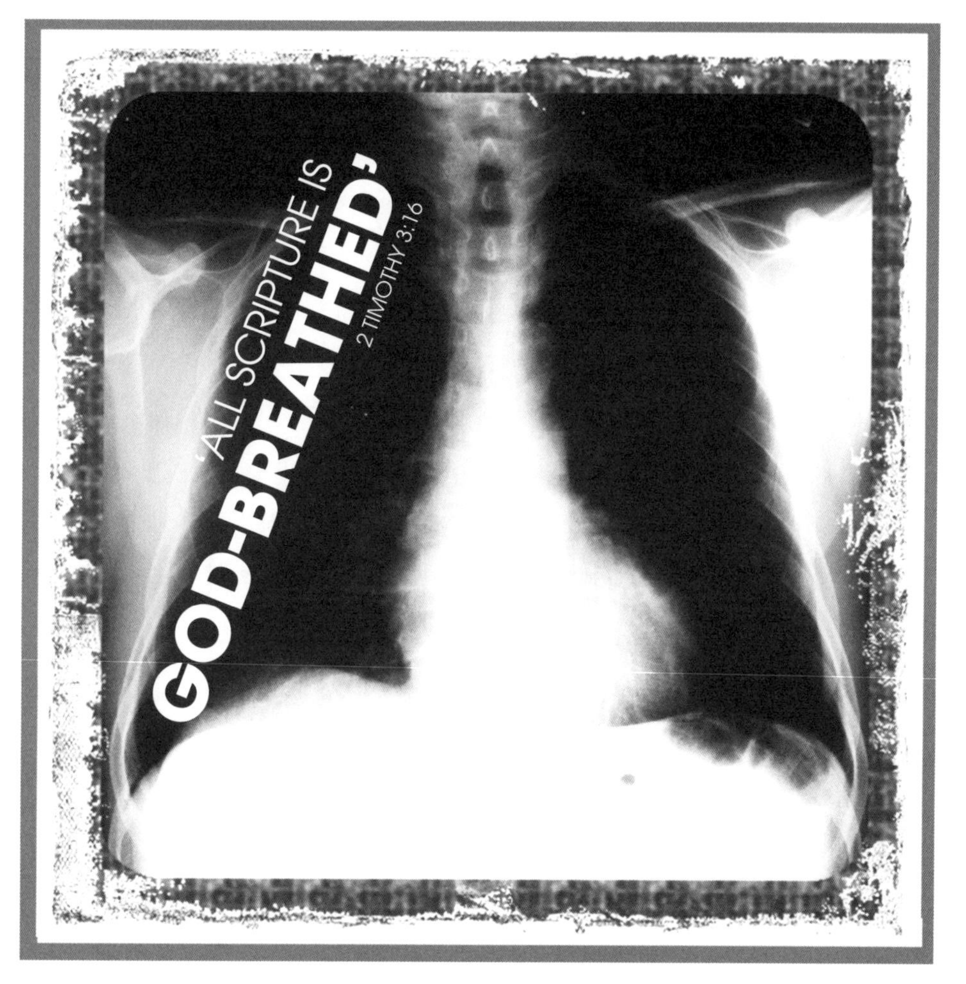
'ALL SCRIPTURE IS
GOD-BREATHED'
2 TIMOTHY 3:16

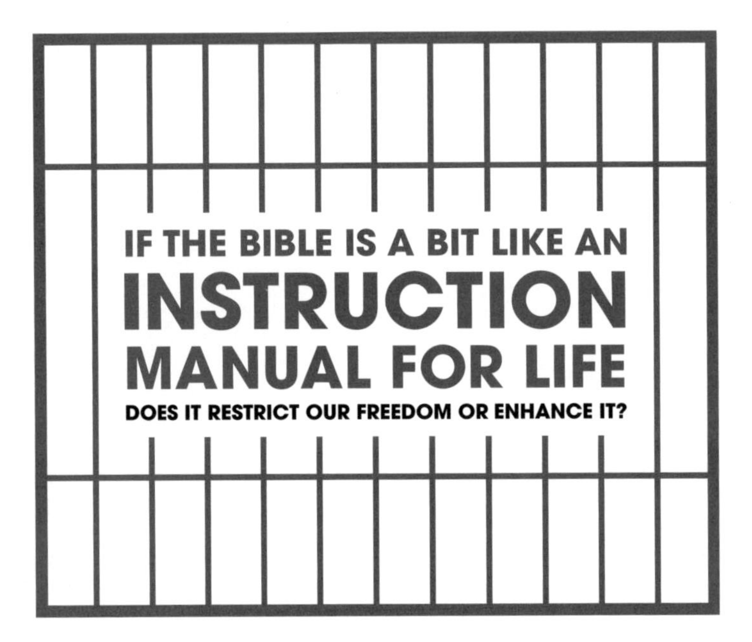
IF THE BIBLE IS A BIT LIKE AN
INSTRUCTION
MANUAL FOR LIFE
DOES IT RESTRICT OUR FREEDOM OR ENHANCE IT?

## Going Deeper: Smuggled Bibles

Nicky Gumbel, the person who pioneered Alpha, told this story:

'My father had always wanted to visit Russia and when he was seventy-three and I was twenty-one we went on a family trip to the Soviet Union. At the time, Christians were being persecuted there and it was very hard to get hold of Bibles, but I took some Christian literature with me, including some Russian Bibles. While I was there I went to churches and looked for people who seemed to be genuine Christians. (At that time the meetings were often infiltrated by the KGB, the Russian Secret Police.)

On one occasion I followed a man, who was in his sixties, down the street after a service. Glancing round to check nobody was there, I went up to him and tapped him on the shoulder. I took out one of my Bibles and handed it to him. For a moment he had an expression of disbelief. Then he took from his pocket a New Testament, which was probably 100 years old, the pages so threadbare they were virtually transparent. When he realised he had received a whole Bible, he was elated. He didn't speak any English, I didn't speak any Russian. We hugged each other and started dancing up and down the street jumping for joy – not something I normally do with someone I have never met, or anyone else for that matter! That man knew that he had in his hands something truly unique.'

# Session 6
# How Does God Guide Us?

# Where do you think you'll be when you are twenty? Or thirty? What decisions will you have to make along the way?

Christians try to follow the guidance of God. Guidance is about figuring out what God is saying to us and following his instructions. God promises to guide us when we ask him.

But God's guidance is not like a set of rules or directions yelled out at us. Instead, it comes out of our relationship with him.

So how does God guide us?

## Through the Bible

- The Bible is full of general guidelines about how we should live our lives and we should always follow these
- If we make a habit of studying the Bible regularly, then God will often bring a particular verse to light at just the right time to help guide us in a decision

## By the Holy Spirit

- The Holy Spirit helps us to recognise God's voice. God speaks to us as we pray – sometimes it's through strong feelings that we just cannot get rid of in our hearts and minds
- Sometimes, God speaks in more extraordinary ways like prophecy, dreams, visions, angels or even an audible voice

## Through common sense & advice from others

- God has given us a conscience and a brain, and he wants us to use them! If something seems like a stupid idea, then it probably is … enough said!
- The wiser you are, the more aware you will be that you need help to make the most of life. Proverbs 15:22 says: 'Plans fail for lack of counsel, but with many advisers they succeed'
- God has given us friends and family to help us make important decisions. We should weigh up their advice

## Through random circumstantial signs

- Our eyes should be open to opportunities and to closed doors (although sometimes we need to keep going in spite of difficulty)
- God sometimes uses 'coincidences' and random stuff to speak to us as well

'Life is what happens to you while you're busy making other plans.'

**'Beautiful Boy', John Lennon, singer and songwriter**

'God wants us to have soft hearts and hard feet. The trouble with so many of us is we have hard hearts and soft feet.'

**Jackie Pullinger, missionary and worker with drug addicts, Hong Kong**

'Everything has been figured out, except how to live.'

**Jean-Paul Sartre, French philosopher and writer**

'FOR I KNOW
THE
PLANS I HAVE FOR
YOU'
DECLARES THE LORD,
'PLANS TO
PROSPER
YOU & NOT TO HARM YOU,
PLANS TO GIVE YOU
HOPE
& A FUTURE.'
JEREMIAH 29:11

HOW DO YOU FEEL ABOUT THE IDEA OF

BEING GUIDED BY GOD?

## Going Deeper: Man 9000

*This true story about the man who set up the Samaritans hotline shows that even random, coincidental events can be used by God to guide us.*

Reverend Chad Varah was the founder of the Samaritans: a telephone hotline which helps and supports people who are in despair or even suicidal. Somebody calls the Samaritans every twenty seconds.

In the early 1950s, Chad Varah was the vicar of a very busy church near Clapham Junction in London. Although he had this idea of a telephone hotline, he didn't think he was the right person to get it started, because he was so busy. So he said to the Lord, 'I'm not the person to do this. I think you need someone from a church in the City' (London's financial district). Churches in the City have very few parishioners, and therefore the vicars have more time available.

A few days later, he was invited to become the vicar of a church exactly like that: the Church of St Stephen's, Walbrook, in the City of London. When he saw the patrons of the church and they asked him what he'd do once he was appointed, he said, 'Well, I'd set up a telephone hotline.' They thought it was a great idea.

On his way to the church, Reverend Varah was thinking: 'What would be the best number for this hotline?' He wanted something that could be easily memorised. He knew that the first three characters would be letters (that was how phone numbers worked back then), so, as the local area was Mansion House, the letters would be M-A-N. He wondered, 'What could the numbers be, in order to give it a hint of emergency? Something like 999.' He decided that the perfect number would be 'MAN 9000' – easily memorable, with a hint of emergency.

He found the church telephone buried under some rubble in the vestry. Once he salvaged it, he dialled the operator and tried to persuade her to give him the phone number 'MAN 9000'.

He asked if it might be possible to change the church's number to 'MAN 9000'. She explained that it was very unlikely: 'Someone with a number as memorable as that wouldn't change it for love nor money.' Reverend Varah said, 'I have no money, but I have plenty of love! Would you tell me who the number "MAN 9000" belongs to so I can contact them myself?'

The operator asked him where he was calling from, and he realised he didn't even know the church's number. He wiped the dust from the phone handset and saw, in clear print, 'MAN 9000'!

After explaining this coincidence to the operator, Reverend Varah said to God, 'I get the message! You had this planned even before the telephone was installed. Now please stop with the coincidences, because it's getting weird!'

# Weekend Session 1
# What About the Holy Spirit?

# The Holy Spirit has often been misunderstood. Who do you think the Holy Spirit is?

Perhaps one of the reasons for not understanding who the Holy Spirit is because we've just never had the chance to see all that he is. Some older versions of the Bible call him the 'Holy Ghost', which sounds a little scary! But the Holy Spirit is not a 'ghost' at all – he is the third person of the Trinity of God – Father, Son and *Holy Spirit*.

## The Holy Spirit throughout the Bible

- The Holy Spirit was involved in creating everything that we see, and even the galaxies we can't see – amazing!
- The Hebrew word for Holy Spirit is 'ruach', which means 'breath'. In Genesis, the Holy Spirit is described as God's breath. He breathes life into things, including us!
- In the Old Testament, God gave his Holy Spirit to particular people at particular times to do particular jobs but God promised that at the right time the Holy Spirit would come in a new way
- After Jesus' resurrection, he promised that his disciples would receive the Holy Spirit. On the day of Pentecost, the disciples were praying together and suddenly the Holy Spirit came and filled them in a completely new way. From there they went out and literally changed the world!

## The Holy Spirit makes us part of God's family

- Isn't it strange how some dogs look like their owners? When we become a Christian, the Holy Spirit makes us part of God's family, and a family likeness begins to show in our character. As we spend time with God we become more like him
- We start a new spiritual life and will grow like God in terms of how we act and live – these characteristics are called the 'fruits of the Spirit' in the Bible

## The Holy Spirit gives us gifts

- The Holy Spirit helps us to understand God, and the Bible and helps us to pray. He gives us the power to live for Jesus and the courage to tell others
- The Holy Spirit gives us spiritual gifts. The Bible tells us about these (1 Corinthians 12) – each of us is given different gifts to help us play our part

An electric plug on its own is fairly useless – it needs to be connected to a power source. God's Spirit is the power source that we, as Christians, can connect to, and not just as a one-off, but all the time.

'There is no deep renewal in our lives unless we open ourselves and let the Spirit come into our lives. He wants to. He wants for us to open the door. I hope this day many of you will open the door to the Holy Spirit.'

**Father Raniero Cantalamessa, Preacher to the Papal Household**

'When you say a prayer, He [the Holy Spirit] is in every word of it, and, like a Holy Fire, penetrates every word of it.'

**Saint John of Kronstadt**

'And I will ask the Father, and he will give you another advocate to help you and to be with you forever – the Spirit of truth'

**John 14:16–17**

'THE FRUIT OF THE SPIRIT IS
love,
joy,
PEACE,
patience,
kindness,
faithfulness,
GOODNESS,
gentleness
and
self-control.
AGAINST SUCH THINGS THERE IS NO LAW.' GALATIANS 5:22-23

DOES THE IDEA OF THE HOLY SPIRIT SEEM **POSITIVE** TO YOU?

## Going Deeper: Who Is The Holy Spirit?

In John 15:26, Jesus says: 'When the Counsellor comes …' The literal Greek word there is *parakletos*, which is a difficult word to translate. Literally, it means 'the one called alongside'. Sometimes it's translated 'the advocate', the one who stands by you in court; sometimes 'the encourager', the one who stands by you to encourage you and at other times, 'the comforter'.

But literally it's 'the one called alongside'. If a little ship was in trouble on the Mediterranean Sea, they would send a big ship alongside it to draw it back to the safety of the harbour. That big ship was called a *parakletos* – 'the one called alongside'.

Some rights reserved by Andrea Guerra

An article in *The Independent* newspaper told the story of a 24-year-old man called Alan Anderson, who was flying in a light aircraft. There was just him and the pilot – but Alan Anderson had absolutely no flying experience. As they were flying, the pilot dropped dead from a heart attack. So there Alan was – no flying experience, on his own, in this light aircraft.

Alan managed to send out a May Day emergency call, and a flying instructor called Robert Legge, responded and caught up with him 2,000 feet above Penarth, near Cardiff.

An amateur radio enthusiast called Howard Day happened to be listening in to their radio conversation as this instructor responded. This is what he heard.

The first thing that Anderson said, when he saw the instructor coming alongside, was, 'I can see you.' To which Legge, the instructor, said, 'Okay, just listen to my instructions. Take the throttle and pull it slightly until the RPM drops down to about 2,300.'

Anderson: 'Well, which is the throttle?'

Legge: 'There should be a black lever in the centre of the panel. That's fine. Let the aeroplane fly itself.'

Anderson: 'I wish it would!'

Legge: 'Read the airspeed.'

Anderson: 'The airspeed's 105!'

Legge: 'Look, I'm on your right-hand side. Just relax.'

Anderson: 'Are we going down?'

Legge: 'We are shortly, yes. Bank gently to the right. We're aiming for the wide tarmac airstrip to the right of the red and white lights. Can you see it?'

Anderson: 'Affirmative.'

Legge: 'Reduce the power slightly now. What's your airspeed?'

Anderson: '100.'

Legge: 'Pull back very gently on the control column. Close the throttle. Just hold it there. Pull gently back and hold it there … hold it … hold it … hold it … hold the control column back. Relax. Okay, on the rudder pedals, press the top of the rudder pedals. You'll find the brakes. Press both rudder pedals together. You'll find the brakes.'

Anderson: 'I can't find the brakes!'

Legge: 'Don't worry. The emergency vehicles are coming up behind you. Just sit in the aircraft. Leave the engine rumbling, turn the keys to OFF, then take them out. The engine should then stop. Has the engine stopped?'

Anderson: 'The keys are out. Just stopping now. Thank God!'

Legge: 'You're welcome, it's all in a day's work.' He had guided him to a near perfect landing.

The article in *The Independent* went on to say: 'Mr. Anderson was last night recovering from deep shock. His mother, Carol Anderson, said he'd vowed never to fly again.'

*Maybe there are things going on in your life – anxieties, fears, situations where you'd love someone to come and help. The Holy Spirit is the one who draws alongside of us, to be the encourager, the comforter, the Counsellor. We just need to ask.*

# Weekend Session 2
# How Can I Be Filled with the Holy Spirit?

# All Christians have the Holy Spirit in them. The question is, how much will we allow the Holy Spirit to fill us?

You might be wondering what it means to be 'full' of the Holy Spirit? Is it the same as becoming a Christian?

All Christians have the Holy Spirit in them, but not all Christians are *filled* with the Holy Spirit.

God doesn't want us to just have a little bit of his Spirit; he wants us to be filled so that we burn brightly, giving off heat and light to those around us.

## What happens when people experience the Holy Spirit?

- In the New Testament, Paul writes 'Be filled with the [Holy] Spirit' (Ephesians 5:18)
- The translation of this means 'go on being filled' so being filled with the Spirit shouldn't just be a one-off experience: Paul wanted everyone to be constantly filled and refilled
- In the Bible, in the Book of Acts, we see that things happen when people are filled with the Spirit (Acts 10:44–46)

- When we are filled with the Spirit, we should focus on Jesus and not just on any physical feelings we may experience
- All of us need to feel love, but we look for the *person* that we love, not the *feeling*. Being filled is about the Spirit leading us into a deeper relationship with the *person* Jesus, it is not an 'end' in itself

## Can anything stop us from being filled?

- God wants to fill all his children with his Holy Spirit, but sometimes we put up barriers that make it difficult for this to happen
- Sometimes we doubt that God will give us his Spirit if we ask – but the Bible says 'everyone who asks shall receive' – and that, includes you and me (Luke 11:9–10)
- Sometimes we get scared that it might not be a good thing – but God is our father and wants to give us good gifts (Luke 11:11–13)
- Sometimes we doubt that we're worthy of the gift – we might think, 'God knows what I'm really like, I'm not holy enough.' But Jesus *doesn't* say, 'How much more will your Father in heaven give the Holy Spirit to really holy people who've been Christians for a very long time and deserve it.' He says: 'How much more will your Father in heaven give the Holy Spirit to those who ask him!' (Luke 11:13). All we have to do is ask him

'I just wanna feel real love'
**Robbie Williams, singer**

Have you ever fallen in love? All of us behave differently when it happens. It would be crazy to focus on the physical effects of falling in love rather than on the actual person we've fallen in love with, wouldn't it?

'Bart, with $10,000, we'd be millionaires! We could buy all kinds of useful things like ... love!'
**Homer Simpson**

EPHESIANS 5:18
'INSTEAD, BE
FILLED
WITH THE
SPIRIT.'

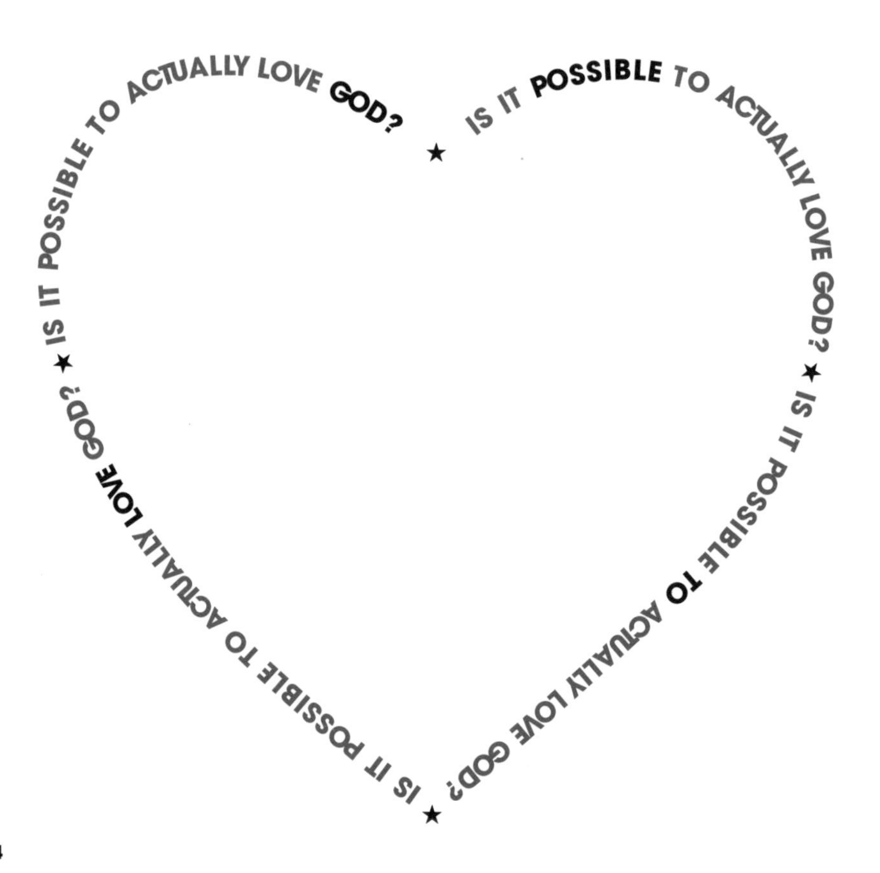
IS IT POSSIBLE TO ACTUALLY LOVE GOD?
IS IT POSSIBLE TO ACTUALLY LOVE GOD?
IS IT POSSIBLE TO ACTUALLY LOVE GOD?
IS IT POSSIBLE TO ACTUALLY LOVE GOD?

## Going Deeper: Shane's Story

From the age of fourteen or fifteen, Shane Taylor carried a knife. He had a fascination with guns and knives – mainly knives. He finally got caught, and the charge was Section 20 – GBH. Shane was nineteen. He got Section 20 for two stabbings, a couple of affrays and carrying offensive weapons. He was sentenced to four years.

In his own words Shane describes himself as 'crazy, doing loads of violent and mad things. I was the madman that everyone looked up to – and I had a gang of people who would do what I asked them to do.'

Shane ended up in a maximum security prison – in the segregation unit and finally in the 'CSC' (Close Supervision Centre) where prisoners who are so dangerous are held and where there can be no physical contact between them and the prison officers.

Whilst in prison, he found himself on Alpha. Here's what he had to say about it:

'My intention wasn't to find God. I was thinking, "Free coffee, chocolate biscuits and gateau!"

I settled down quite quickly and began to turn up to each of the sessions. I was mostly interested in getting the chocolate biscuits and having little debates, saying things like, "Science proves that it's wrong …"

Eventually we got to the Holy Spirit day. After we'd watched the videos and had our discussion everyone sat down and we each got prayed for.

The minister, Eddie Baker, put his hand on my head and prayed for me but nothing particularly happened.

Later on I was making a cup of coffee when he came up to me and said, "I've never done this in all the years I've worked here, but I think God is telling me to tell you to come back here this afternoon."

I said, "All right then, I'll come." I remember saying to myself, "If it's real then prove it." I went to the church that afternoon and Eddie was there waiting for me.

He picked up a Bible and opened up a few verses where it said something like, "Jesus Christ died on a cross for you. He died for your sins and you can be forgiven."

Then Eddie put his hand on my head and prayed for me. Then he took his hand off and said, "Now you pray."

I said, "What about?"

And he said, "From your heart – let it out and pray."

I said, "Jesus Christ, I know you died on a cross for me. Please, I don't like who I am, please forgive me, please." I said a few other things, which I can't remember now. And then I sat back and we started talking.

As I talked I started to feel a weird feeling in my belly. I thought, "What's that?" But I kept talking to him. Then I started to feel this bubbly feeling slowly coming up my body – through my legs, my chest. When it got to about halfway I started to feel tears coming into my eyes.

I tried to hold it back. I stopped talking, thinking that was going to stop it, because I didn't want to cry. Here I was, a hard man in prison – I didn't want to cry.

But it rose up and up and up until suddenly I began crying my eyes out. I hadn't cried in years. I cried for about five minutes and I could feel a weight being lifted off me because I felt light. Eddie said in a nice voice, "That's the Holy Spirit. It's Jesus."'

Shane attends a local church with his wife Sam. They have two daughters, Angel and Grace. Shane says 'I never believed God would give me a lovely family. God is great.'

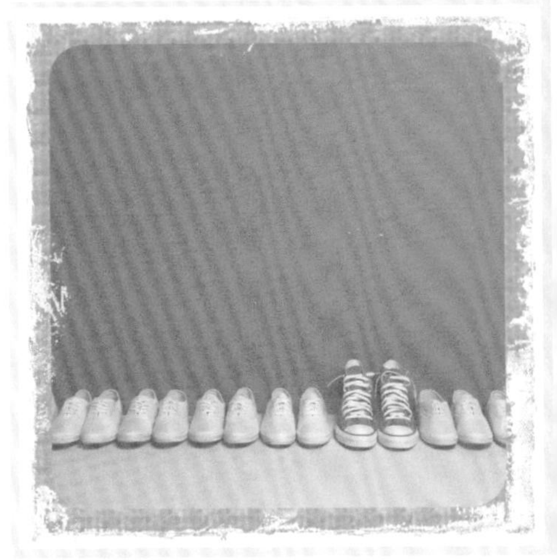

# Weekend Session 3
# How Can I Make the Most of the Rest of My Life?

# Is life about *existing* or is it about *living*?

We only get one shot at life, no matter who we are. As the saying goes, 'Life is not a dress rehearsal.'

## So what should we do?

- The amazing, yet strange, thing about the kingdom of God is that it seems upside-down in comparison to the world. Following Jesus involves living counter-culturally – living differently to the culture around us
- It is tough living for God in today's world, especially at school. It can be easy to let pressure from the world squeeze and force us to 'fit the mould' of everyone else
- The way to make the most of our lives is to offer them to God

## So how do we 'live differently'?

- The secret is to let God transform us from the inside out
- We can pray to God and offer all areas of our life to him: our time, our ambitions, our dreams, our money, our sexuality, what we watch, what we say, what we do ...
- If we do this, we will maximise life, not lose it
- Of course, this is not the easiest way to live, but Jesus promises
  to be with us and give us life (John 10:10)

## Why should we offer our lives to God?

- God has a great plan for our future – he wants the best for us. The simple truth is that if we live for Jesus, then we will not miss out on life – in fact, our lives will be as full as they could possibly be
- Jesus said, 'Seek first the kingdom of God… and all these things will be given to you' (Matthew 6:33)
- God has done great things for us – we owe it to him

'If you live to be a hundred, I want to live to be a hundred minus one day, so I never have to live without you.'
**A. A. Milne, Winnie the Pooh**

'The next moment is as much beyond our grasp, and as much in God's care, as that a hundred years away. Care for the next minute is as foolish as care for a day in the next thousand years. In neither can we do anything, in both God is doing everything.'
**C. S. Lewis, author of the 'Narnia' books**

'Sing like no one's listening, love like you've never been hurt, dance like nobody's watching, and live like it's heaven on earth.'
**Mark Twain, American author**

'Do not conform any longer to the pattern of this world... but be transformed by the renewing of your mind.'
**Romans 12:2**

HEBREWS 12:1
'LET US THROW OFF EVERYTHING THAT HINDERS
AND THE SIN THAT SO EASILY ENTANGLES,
AND LET US
RUN
WITH PERSEVERANCE
THE RACE MARKED OUT
FOR US.'

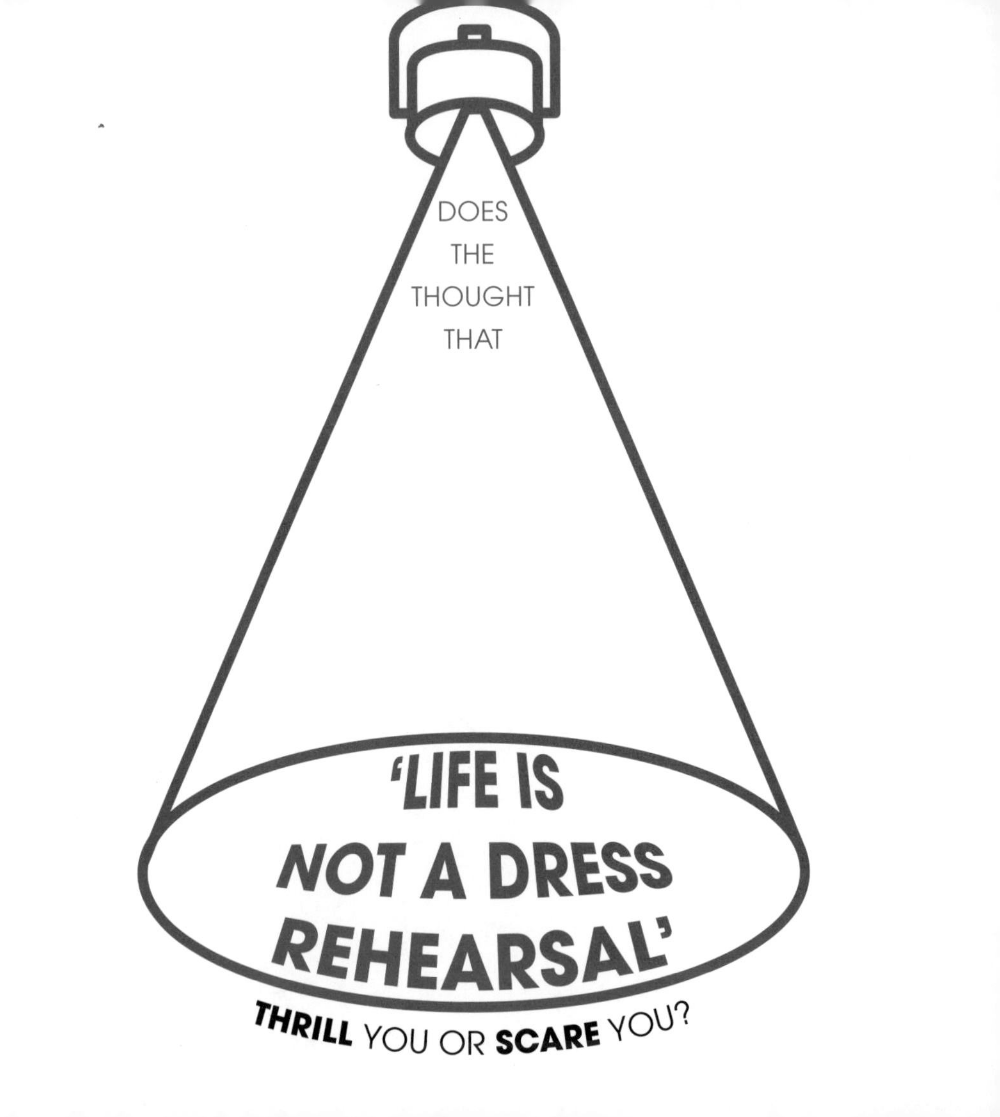
DOES
THE
THOUGHT
THAT
'LIFE IS
NOT A DRESS
REHEARSAL'
THRILL YOU OR SCARE YOU?

## Going Deeper: Peer Pressure

In the 1950s, a very famous experiment was done by a guy called Solomon Asch (you can check it out on YouTube). It was designed to test how easily people would go along with the rest of a group. Asch put people into groups of five (four actors and one non-actor), showed them four lines on a page and asked them which two lines were the same length. The actors were told to give the same, wrong answer. Seventy-five per cent of the non-actors went with the group and gave the same wrong answer, even though it was blatantly incorrect!

Often, it is much easier to blend in and go along with what everyone else is doing, even when it is obviously wrong.

# Session 7
# How Can I Resist Evil?

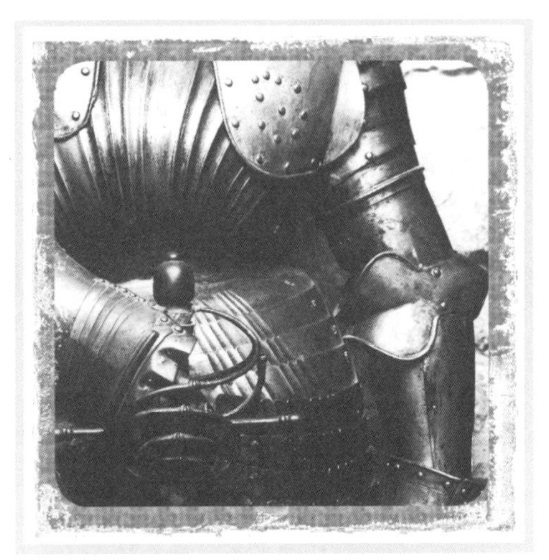

# Is evil a reality in our world? Where does it come from?

Have you ever noticed that if you add one letter to the word 'God' you get 'good'? If you add one letter to the word 'evil' you get 'devil'. The claim of the New Testament is that, just as behind goodness lies God himself, behind the evil in the world lies the devil.

## Why should we believe that the devil exists?

- It is clear from the horror and evil in our world that he is at work
- Christians have believed in his existence down the ages
- The Bible speaks of him in the Old Testament and in the New Testament
- But beware – taking too much of an interest in the devil is just as dangerous as doubting that he even exists

## What has the devil got to do with me?

- The Bible tells us that there is a kind of spiritual war going on that we can't see (Ephesians 6:11–12)
- The devil's aim is to steal our freedom and destroy us (John 10:10). He wants to prevent us from having a proper relationship with God, and will do anything he can to stop this

- The devil's tactics are to create doubt in our minds, cause us to take our eyes off Jesus and tempt us to sin

## Should we be worried?

- No! Jesus is all powerful and he has set us free. We have all the forces of heaven on our side, so we have nothing to fear
- On the cross, Jesus won the war and has completely defeated Satan but there are still battles going on, and as soldiers in God's army, we are involved in these (Luke 10:17–20)

## So how do we attack?

- By praying – the Bible says that 'The weapons we fight with are not the weapons of the world. On the contrary, they have divine power to demolish strongholds' (2 Corinthians 10:4)
- By action – we attack the devil by doing the things that Jesus told us to do (Luke 7:22)
- We can also defend ourselves by putting on the 'full armour of God' (see page 101)

WHY DO YOU THINK THE WORLD IS IN SUCH A
MESS?

## Putting on the armour of God

The Bible says: 'Finally, be strong in the Lord and in his mighty power. Put on the full armour of God, so that you can take your stand against the devil's schemes. For our struggle is not against flesh and blood, but against the rulers, against the authorities, against the powers of this dark world and against the spiritual forces of evil in the heavenly realms. Therefore put on the full armor of God, so that when the day of evil comes, you may be able to stand your ground, and after you have done everything, to stand. Stand firm then, with the belt of truth buckled around your waist, with the breastplate of righteousness in place, and with your feet fitted with the readiness that comes from the gospel of peace. In addition to all this, take up the shield of faith, with which you can extinguish all the flaming arrows of the evil one. Take the helmet of salvation and the sword of the Spirit, which is the word of God.' (Ephesians 6:10–17)

That's six practical pieces of God's armour for defending ourselves:

1. Focus on Jesus – 'the belt of truth'. We can know Jesus' truth, which counters the devil's lies.
2. Keep your relationships right – 'the breastplate of righteousness'. Keep short accounts with God and with other people.
3. Get involved in serving God – 'the boots of the gospel of peace'. Tell others about the good news of Jesus.
4. Keep trusting God – 'the shield of faith'. Be sure of God's promises.
5. Protect your mind – 'the helmet of salvation'. Watch what we fill our minds with.
6. Know your Bible – 'the sword of the Spirit'. Get to know the Bible and attack the devil with its truth.

'As far as God goes, I'm a non-believer. But when it comes to the devil – well, that's something else. The devil keeps advertising; the devil does lots of commercials.'

**William Peter Blatty, writer and producer of The Exorcist**

'Good can exist without evil, whereas evil cannot exist without good.'

**Thomas Aquinas, philosopher and theologian**

'There are two equal and opposite errors into which we can fall about the devils. One is to disbelieve in their existence; the other is to believe and to feel an excessive and unhealthy interest in them. They themselves are equally pleased by both errors.'

**C. S. Lewis, author of the 'Narnia' books**

'DO NOT BE OVERCOME BY EVIL,
BUT
OVERCOME EVIL
WITH
GOOD.'
ROMANS 12:21

## Going Deeper: The Story of Corrie ten Boom

Corrie ten Boom was a Dutch Christian Holocaust survivor, imprisoned in the Nazi concentration camps during World War II because she and her family had been hiding Jews and helping them escape from the Nazis. One of the concentration camps that she and her sister, Betsie, were imprisoned in was called Ravensbruck. Betsie died in this concentration camp.

After the war, Corrie spoke about her experience all round the world. Here is what happened to her on one such occasion:

'It was at a church service in Munich that I saw him, a former S.S. man who had stood guard at the shower room door in the processing center at Ravensbruck. He was the first of our actual jailers that I had seen since that time. And suddenly it was all there – the roomful of mocking men, the heaps of clothing, Betsie's pain-blanched face.

He came up to me as the church was emptying, beaming and bowing. "How grateful I am for your message, Fraulein."

He said. "To think that, as you say, He has washed my sins away!" His hand was thrust out to shake mine. And I, who had preached so often to the people in Bloemendaal the need to forgive, kept my hand at my side.

Even as the angry, vengeful thoughts boiled through me, I saw the sin of them. Jesus Christ had died for this man; was I going to ask for more? "Lord Jesus", I prayed, "forgive me and help me to forgive him." I tried to smile, I struggled to raise my hand. I could not. I felt nothing, not the slightest spark of warmth or charity. And so again I breathed a silent prayer. "Jesus", I prayed, "I cannot forgive him. Give me your forgiveness."

As I took his hand the most incredible thing happened. From my shoulder along my arm and through my hand a current seemed to pass from me to him, while into my heart sprang a love for this stranger that almost overwhelmed me. And so I discovered that it is not on our forgiveness any more than on our goodness that the world's healing hinges, but on His. When He tells us to love our enemies, He gives – along with the command, the love itself.'

(Adapted from ecclesia.org/truth/corrie.html)

# Session 8
# Why and How Should I Tell Others?

# What do you do when you hear good news?

## Why should we tell other people about our faith in Jesus?

**Reason 1** Because Jesus told us to. After he rose again from the dead, he said to go and tell everyone the amazing news: that you can be forgiven; you can be set free; you can have eternal life.

**Reason 2** Because we love our friends and family. Love must be what motivates us, because we want people to discover what we have found in Jesus.

**Reason 3** Because it is good news! We can't just keep it to ourselves.

- Right from the start it is good to recognise two possible extremes: either trying to force our views down other people's throats or going silent and never telling anyone about our faith
- The key to avoiding these two mistakes is to really care about the person you are telling, and to trust God

## How can we share our faith?

- **Live the message:** When people know that we are Christians, they will watch how we live. Our actions should match our words. We are called by God to love those around us, to love the poor and stand up against injustice
- **Talk the message:**
  - If we live like Christians it is quite likely that people will notice and want us to talk about it. There is no formula for how to speak about your faith – the important thing is to tell your story and be natural. Never use force and don't pressurise people
  - If you don't know the answer to a question, don't worry, and don't pretend you do! Just be willing to go away and find out. Some questions are so big they have lots of books written on them and still no one has an absolute answer for them
- **Present the message:** It is easy to think, 'What difference could I make?' But we are all called to tell what we've experienced of God
- **Trust the message:** God still does miracles today, and we shouldn't be afraid to ask him to show his power to people
- **Pray the message:** Prayer is the power behind any attempt to tell people the good news about Jesus. If we haven't been praying, then we shouldn't necessarily expect to see anything happen. We can pray that people's eyes would be opened to the truth about God and that God would give us boldness to talk about our faith (Acts 4:29–31)

'On our last day at the orphanage, a man handed me his baby and said, "Take him with you." He knew in Ireland his son would live; in Ethiopia his son would die. I turned him down. In that moment, I started this journey. In that moment I became the worst thing of all: a rock-star with a cause. Except this isn't a cause – 6,500 Africans dying a day of treatable, preventable disease, dying for want of medicines you and I can get at our local chemist: that's not a cause; that's an emergency.'

**Bono, lead singer of U2**

The word 'go' appears 1,514 times in the Bible. In the New Testament it appears 233 times, in Matthew's Gospel it's 54 times. Jesus says, 'Go and tell… Go and invite… Go and make disciples'.

'Preach the gospel at all times; if necessary, use words.'

**Saint Francis of Assisi**

'Evangelisation must touch people's minds and hearts, stir their consciences and engage all their energies.'

**Pope John Paul II**

HE HAS SENT ME
TO BIND UP THE
BROKEN-HEARTED,
TO PROCLAIM
FREEDOM
FOR THE CAPTIVES AND
RELEASE
FROM
DARKNESS
FOR THE
PRISONERS
ISAIAH 61:1

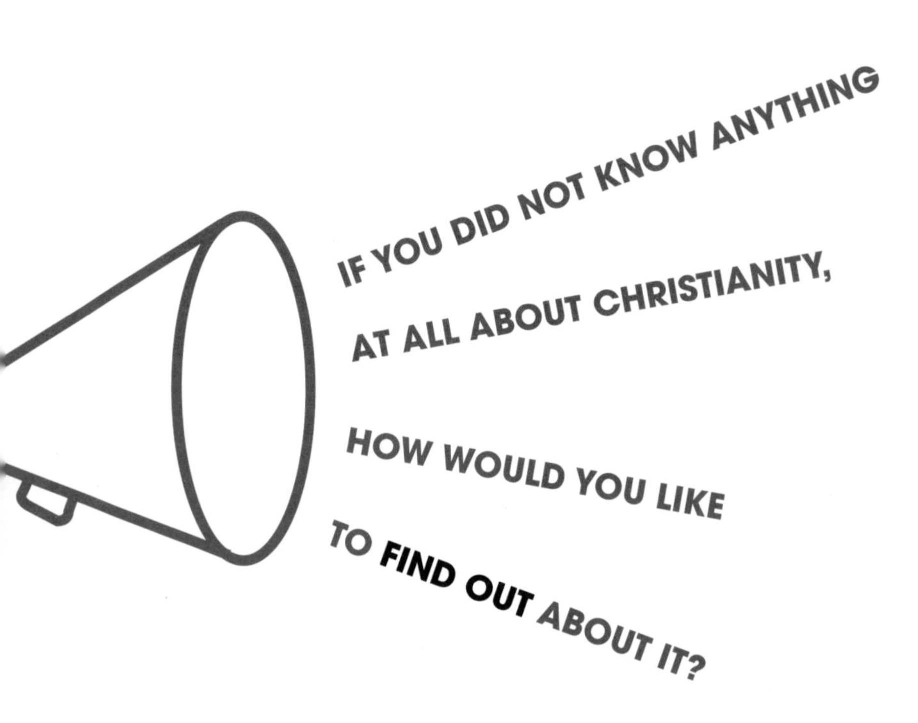
IF YOU DID NOT KNOW ANYTHING
AT ALL ABOUT CHRISTIANITY,
HOW WOULD YOU LIKE
TO FIND OUT ABOUT IT?

## Going Deeper: One Starfish at a Time

A man was walking along a beach in Mexico when he saw a remarkable sight – the beach was covered in tens of thousands of starfish! The tide had gone out and left them stranded on the beach, dying in the heat of the sun. The man saw a young boy standing among the starfish. The boy was picking them up one at a time, running down to the sea and throwing them into the water, before going back to get another starfish and repeating the process again.

The man went up to him and said, 'Look, can't you see — there are tens of thousands of starfish out here! I don't really think what you're doing is going to make any difference.'

The young boy picked up another starfish, went down to the water's edge, threw it in the sea and said, 'I bet it made a difference for that one!'

*We may not be able to change the world on our own, but we can change the lives of those around us, one by one.*

*Could you try doing one of these in the next week?*

- *praying for a friend*
- *asking a friend to a youth event at your church*
- *making an effort to talk to a lonely or bullied person at school*
- *asking God to give you the opportunity to tell somebody the story of how you came to be a Christian*

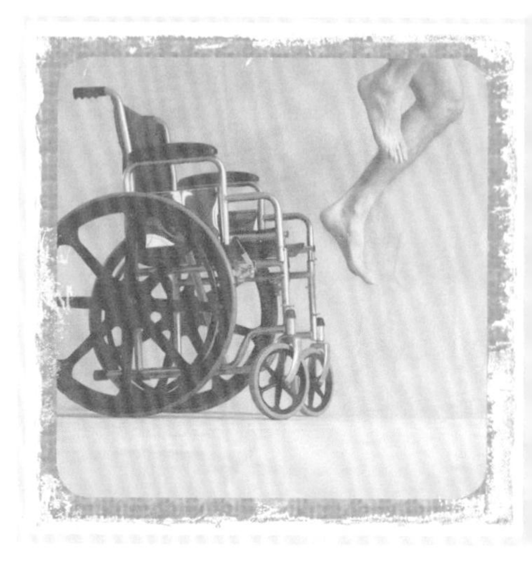

# Session 9
# Does God Heal Today?

# Do you believe that God can heal people today?

## Healing in the Bible

- If we read the Bible, especially the Gospels, we see a God who heals. Twenty-five percent of the Gospels are about healing!
- God promised to heal his people in the Old Testament. He says, 'I am the God who heals you' (Exodus 15:26). It is his nature to heal
- Jesus sent his disciples out to pray for healing. He gave them authority to heal the sick in his name. As Jesus went up to heaven, he commissioned his disciples – and that includes all of us – to go and do as he did (Matthew 28:16–20)
- That's exactly what the disciples did – they preached the gospel and healed the sick. They believed that the two went side by side

## Healing in history

- The earliest churches believed healing was possible and they acted on that. But it didn't stop there – the church has been praying for the sick and seeing God perform miracles ever since

## How do we pray for healing?

- Our job is to pray – it is God who does the healing
- Our prayers for healing should be simple, not long and complicated. Remember, it is God's power, not our words, that heal
- We need to check our motive – Jesus healed people because he loved them. It is important that we care and want the best for anyone we pray for
- We should not give up if nothing seems to happen or if the person is only partially healed. Jesus sometimes had to pray twice, so we shouldn't feel discouraged at having to do so
- The kingdom of God is the key to understanding our experience of healing in the world today – it is both 'now' and 'not yet'. That means that when Jesus came to earth, he brought the kingdom of God. The healings he did were a sign that the kingdom of God had arrived, but it hasn't yet arrived in its completeness. Where healing doesn't happen we are reminded that we still have to wait to see the kingdom come fully

God can heal our bodies, and he can also heal other types of hurts too, whether it's emotional pain or any other kind of pain. Nothing is impossible for God.

'God does not give, or even allow, sickness in order to teach us something. However, he turns all things for good for those who love him. So if you are sick, ask God what he wants to teach you through it and how you can bless others as a result. The devil is the author of sickness and his plan is to make you blame God and turn from him and make you focus on yourself and your sickness and how unfair it all is. Pray and seek your healing from the living God who heals. It's part of his DNA to heal, so praying these prayers are in line with his character – but be patient, and persistent, pursuing him, as his timing is very often different to ours. Seek first *his* kingdom.'

PATRICK PEARSON-MILES has 'chronic renal failure' which basically means his kidneys don't work at all – he hasn't had a pee since 1994! He developed kidney disease aged seventeen; ten years later his kidneys packed up.

'I AM
THE
LORD,
WHO
HEALS
YOU.'
EXODUS 15:26

WHY
DO
YOU
THINK
JESUS
HEALED
PEOPLE
?

## Going Deeper 1: Ajay's Story

Ajay Gohill was born in Kenya but moved to England in 1971. He was brought up as a Hindu and worked in the family business as a newsagent in Neasden. At the age of twenty-one he contracted Erythrodermic Psoriasis, a chronic skin disease. His weight dropped from 11.5 [73 kg] to 7.5 stone [47.5 kg]. He was treated all over the world – in the United States, Germany, Switzerland and Israel, as well as all over England. He said that he spent eighty per cent of his earnings trying to find a cure and he took strong drugs which affected his liver. Eventually, he had to give up his job. The disease covered his body from head to toe; he was so horrible to look at, he couldn't even wear a t-shirt. He lost all his friends, and his wife and son left him. He wanted to die.

One October, Ajay was lying in his hospital bed. He cried out, 'God, if you are watching, let me die – I am sorry if I have done something wrong.' From his locker he pulled out a Good News Bible. He opened it at random and read Psalm 38:

*'O Lord, don't punish me in your anger! You have wounded me with your arrows; you have struck me down. Because of your anger, I am in great pain; my whole body is diseased because of my sins. I am drowning in the flood of my sins; they are a burden*

*too heavy to bear. Because I have been foolish, my sores stink and rot. I am bowed down, I am crushed; I mourn all day long. I am burning with fever and I am near to death. I am worn out and utterly crushed; my heart is troubled and I groan with pain. O Lord, you know what I long for; you hear all my groans. My heart is pounding, my strength is gone, and my eyes have lost their brightness. My friends and neighbours will not come near me, because of my sores; even my family keeps away from me… Do not abandon me, O God; do not stay away from me, my God! Help me now, O Lord my saviour!'* (Psalm 38:1–11, 21–22, Good News Bible).

Each and every verse seemed relevant to him. He prayed for God to heal him, and then he fell into a deep sleep. When he awoke the next morning 'everything looked new'. He took a bath and when he looked at the water, he saw the skin had lifted off his body and was floating. He called in the nurses and told them that God was healing him: all of his skin was new, like a baby's. He was totally healed and has since been reunited with his son. Ajay says that the inner healing that has taken place in his life is even greater than the physical healing. He says, 'Every day I live for Jesus. I am his servant today.'

## Going Deeper 2: Ali's Story

Between the ages of about fifteen to nineteen, I had around thirty-three warts on my right hand. Some were quite painful. They were really quite visible and obvious on my hand and I was super-aware of them. I tried everything to get them to go, from creams to having them painfully iced at the doctors, but they never seemed to budge.

I remember my mum saying she'd like to pray for them but I remember also getting quite annoyed with her and saying what difference would that make, didn't she realise how painful and deep rooted they were? I didn't really believe in the reality of God then and am certainly sure I didn't believe in the power of prayer.

I went on my gap year and the people at my work during that time even teased me and called me 'leper', refusing to shake my hand sometimes, all in jest but it definitely got to me after a while…

That summer, at the end of my gap year, I went on a trip with the youth group I was loosely involved with, to Tanzania, Africa, which was really eye-opening and great fun. Because of work commitments I had to come back a week earlier than all the other young people. Halfway through that week, I woke up one day and over the course of the day was able to just peel my warts off my hand with no pain. It was almost as if there was some special liquid on them and by the

end of the day they'd all come off. What was awesome was that the next day it was almost as if they'd not been there at all, no scars...

I thought it was cool and when the youth group came back, including my sixteen-year-old sister, I mentioned to her that, 'by the way my warts have all gone'.

She said to me that she'd really felt that she should pray for my warts while out in Africa, and had got the whole youth group together to pray, and lo and behold at the same time, the same week, they'd all come off my hand.

I dismissed it as coincidence but I remember her challenging me and saying that no, this time I couldn't just dismiss it, that she felt it was God showing how real and powerful he was to me. For the first time in my life, I think I truly believed in a God who was real, powerful and able to change things in my life, and a God who heard our prayers and had the power to heal.

# Session 10
# What About the Church?

# What is the church? Just another club? A type of building? Somewhere to waste a couple of hours on a Sunday morning? Or is it much, much more?

Many people think church is mind-numbingly boring and totally pointless.

This is a shame, as Jesus was passionate about the church! The New Testament is packed full of images of what the church should be like. Here are a few:

## The people of God

- The Bible tells us that the 'church' is made up of people, not buildings (1 Peter 2:9)
- Being a Christian is about having a relationship with God, but it is also about having relationships with other people. It's a great idea to join a church and to be part of a Christian youth group so we can build those relationships

## The family of God

- Jesus' prayer before he died was that we would all be one – that we would all be united, unified (John 17:11)
- Have you heard the saying 'You can choose your friends but you can't choose your family'? It's the same with church – we may be very different but we are called to love one another
- Sometimes family members argue. It's the same in the church – denominations do not always agree. But we are all still part of God's family

## The body of Christ

- Just as different parts of the body have their own functions, we are all given different gifts by God to use in the church. Together we form the body of Christ, united by the Holy Spirit
- The Bible uses this example: 'The eye cannot say to the hand, "I don't need you!" And the head cannot say to the feet, "I don't need you!" ' (1 Corinthians 12:21) – we all need each other, we all have different roles to play
- We can ask God to show us our gifts so we can play our part in the body of Christ

Today the church is huge – it consists of over 2 billion people, which is a third of the world's population

'If all the people who fell asleep in church on Sunday morning were laid out end to end… they would be a great deal more comfortable.'

**Abraham Lincoln, president of the USA 1861-1865**

'How can we live in harmony? First we need to know we are all madly in love with the same God.'

**Thomas Aquinas, philosopher and theologian**

'BUT YOU ARE A
CHOSEN PEOPLE,
A ROYAL
PRIESTHOOD,
A HOLY NATION,
A PEOPLE
BELONGING
TO GOD,
THAT YOU MAY DECLARE THE PRAISES
OF HIM WHO CALLED YOU
OUT OF DARKNESS
INTO HIS
WONDERFUL
LIGHT.
ONCE YOU WERE NOT A PEOPLE,
BUT NOW YOU ARE THE PEOPLE
OF GOD.'
1 PETER 2:9

WHAT
PART
ARE
YOU
GOING
TO
PLAY
IN
GOD'S
CHURCH?

## Going Deeper: Coals in a Fire

A young man was really struggling with his Christian faith. He found himself drifting away from the church and from God. He had many doubts and difficulties and was starting to lose his faith. He went to see an older man for advice. They sat down by a big fireplace and started to chat about life.

The young man explained how he was feeling. The older man didn't say anything; instead, he stood up, went over to the fire and picked up the tongs. He took a red-hot coal out of the fire, and put it on the ground in front of the fireplace. As the young man talked, he watched the coal go from red-hot to black, dark and cold.

The older man took the tongs again and put the coal back in the fire. Within a few minutes the coal was red-hot again. He didn't need to say anything. The young man left knowing exactly why his faith had gone a bit cold.

*It's the same with our Christian lives. If we get involved with church, our faith can stay 'hot' for Jesus. If we don't connect to other Christians, however, we may become discouraged and our faith may become cold.*

# Prayer of Commitment

## The Judge and His Friend

There once were two little boys who were best friends. They played together, went to school together, they even went to university together. They were inseparable, until their careers took them in very different directions.

One became a lawyer, the other a criminal. While one eventually became a judge, the other disappeared deeper and deeper into a life of crime. Eventually the criminal was caught and sent to trial.

On the fateful day in the courtroom, he came face to face with his old best friend, the judge.

So the judge had a dilemma. He loved his friend but he had to do justice.

So the judge handed down the appropriate penalty for the offence – a huge fine.
There was no way that his old friend could ever afford to pay what he owed.

But then the judge took off his robes, went down, stood with his friend, and wrote out a cheque covering the cost.

He paid the penalty himself.

That, in a way, is a bit like us and God. God loves us, but at the same time, there needed to be a price paid for our sin. God can't just say (as that judge couldn't just say), 'It's okay, don't worry about it.' But he paid the penalty himself – through Jesus.

Jesus' death on the cross took away our sin and made us clean again.

It means that God is no longer separated from us, and we can begin a relationship with him.

'For God so loved the world that he gave his one and only Son, that whoever believes in him shall not perish but have eternal life' (John 3:16).

If you feel that you would like to ask Jesus to come into your life and to forgive your sins, then here is a short prayer that you can say.

*Lord Jesus Christ, thank you for dying for me on the cross. I'm sorry for the things in my life that have been wrong. I now turn away from everything that I know is wrong and I now receive your gift of forgiveness. I put my trust in what you did on the cross for me. Please come and fill me with your Holy Spirit and give me the strength to lead the kind of life that deep down I'm longing to lead. Thank you, Lord Jesus. Amen.*

Enjoyed Alpha?
Why not run it for your friends?
Everything you need is at

**alpha.org**